Antarctic Expedition

By Katy Lennon

Penguin
Random
House

Series Editor Deborah Lock
US Senior Editor Shannon Beatty
Project Editor Camilla Gersh
Editor Katy Lennon, Nandini Gupta
Designer Emma Hobson
Art Editor Jyotsna Julka
Illustrator David Buisan
Art Director Martin Wilson
Producer, Pre-production Francesca Wardell

DTP Designers Sachin Gupta, Vijay Kandwal
Picture Researcher Sakshi Saluja
Managing Editor Soma B. Chowdhury
Managing Art Editor Ahlawat Gunjan

Reading Consultant
Linda B. Gambrell, Ph.D.

Subject Consultant
Jamie Oliver,
British Antarctic Survey

First American Edition, 2015
Published in the United States by DK Publishing
345 Hudson Street, New York, New York 10014

Copyright © 2015 Dorling Kindersley Limited
A Penguin Random House Company
15 16 17 18 19 10 9 8 7 6 5 4 3 2 1
001—270532—Sept/15

The publisher would like to thank the following for their kind permission to reproduce their photographs:
(Key: a-above; b-below/bottom; c-center; f-far; l-left; r-right; t-top)
1 Courtesy of the National Science Foundation: August Allen (cl); Jack Green. 8-9 NASA: Michael Studinger (b). 12 Corbis: Ecoscene/
Robert Weight (b). 14 Alamy Images: Danita Delimont (c). 16 Courtesy of the National Science Foundation: August Allen (cl). 16-17
Courtesy of the National Science Foundation: Jack Green (b). 19 Courtesy of the National Science Foundation: Peter Rejcek (t). 20
Courtesy of the National Science Foundation: August Allen (ca); Sean Loutitt (c). 20–21 Dreamstime.com: Luminis. 21 Courtesy of the
National Science Foundation: Elaine Hood (t). 24–25 Courtesy of the National Science Foundation: Peter Rejcek (b). 27 Getty Images:
Fred Hirschmann. 29 Corbis: Arctic-Images (b). 30 Courtesy of the National Science Foundation: Vasilii Petrenko (t). 31 Courtesy of
the National Science Foundation: Chad Naughton (b). 32 Alamy Images: Ashley Cooper (b). 34–35 Corbis: Ann Hawthorne (b). 36 Getty
Images: Photographer's Choice RF/Frank Krahmer (cr); Courtesy of the National Science Foundation: Ken Klassy (clb). 36–37 Courtesy of
the National Science Foundation: Corey Anthony. 37 Courtesy of the National Science Foundation: Madison McConnell (tr). 38–39
Courtesy of the National Science Foundation: Reinhart Piuk. 40 Courtesy of the National Science Foundation: Vasilii Petrenko (cl); Peter
Rejcek (bl). 41 Courtesy of the National Science Foundation: Heidi Roop (bl); Emily Stone (cl). 43 Corbis: 68/Steve Wisbauer/Ocean (br).
44 Corbis: Ann Hawthorne (c). 45 Corbis: Klaus Mellenthin (c). 46 Alamy Images: Nigel Spooner (tr); Christine Whitehead (bl). 47 Getty
Images: Sue Flood (b). 48–49 Alamy Images: All Canada Photos (b). 50 Corbis: Paul A. Souders (l). 51 Corbis: Epa/Yonhap News (b).
52–53 Courtesy of the National Science Foundation: Peter Rejcek (b). 55 Courtesy of the National Science Foundation: Kurtis Burmeister
(cra); Patrick Rowe (tl, tc); Dave Munroe (tr); Zee Evans (ca). 58 Corbis: Richard Morrell (br). 63 Alamy Images: D. Hurst (b); Getty
Images: George C. Beresford (clb); Haynes Archive/Popperfoto (crb). 64 Alamy Images: M&N (cr). 65 Alamy Images: Atomic (br); Sergey
Komarov-Kohl (bl). 67 Alamy Images: Zvonimir Atletic (bl); Classic Image (c). 69 Courtesy of the National Science Foundation: Elaine
Hood. 71 Corbis: Stringer/Reuters. 73 Getty Images: (b). 76–77 Courtesy of the National Science Foundation: Michael Hoffman (b). 76-77
Getty Images: Danita Delimont. 79 Corbis: YONHAP/epa (b). 80 Corbis: Bettmann (br); Hulton-Deutsch Collection (cr). 80–81 Courtesy
of the National Science Foundation: Robyn Waserman (t). 81 Corbis: Bettmann (br). Getty Images: George C. Beresford (cr). 82 Alamy
Images: Heritage Image Partnership Ltd (br). 83 Courtesy of the National Science Foundation: Jennifer Heldmann (bl). 85 Alamy Images:
WW (tr). 86 Dreamstime.com: Sabri Deniz Kizil (cl, bl). 87 Corbis: Bettmann; Hulton-Deutsch Collection (br). Courtesy of the National
Science Foundation: Deven Stross (cr). 90 Alamy Images: Frans Lanting Studio (bl). Courtesy of the National Science Foundation: August
Allen (t); Sven Lidstrom (c, b); Peter Rejcek (cr). 91 Alamy Images: Radharc Images (clb). Courtesy of the National Science Foundation:
Dave Grisez (tr); Sven Lidstrom (t, c). 93 Corbis: James Leynse (b). 95 Corbis: Image Source (b). 97 Courtesy of the National Science
Foundation: Mike Usher (b). 98 Courtesy of the National Science Foundation: Emily Stone (b). 100–101 Getty Images: Carsten Peter (b).
102–103 Courtesy of the National Science Foundation: Dr. Paul Ponganis. 104 Courtesy of the National Science Foundation: Ken Klassy
(cr). 105 Corbis: Momatiuk-Eastcott (tr). 106–107 Courtesy of the National Science Foundation: Peter Rejcek (b). 109 Courtesy of the
National Science Foundation: Reed Scherer. 110–111 Getty Images: Cliff Leight (b). 112-113 Courtesy of the National Science
Foundation: August Allen (b). 117 Courtesy of the National Science Foundation: Liesl Schernthanner (bc); Deven Stross (br); Nick Strehl
(bl). 118 Corbis: Stringer/Reuters (cb). Courtesy of the National Science Foundation: Jaime Ramos (clb). 119 Courtesy of the National
Science Foundation: Corey Anthony (cl); Deven Stross (br); Peter Rejcek (cb). 122 Alamy Images: Zvonimir Atletic (cla); M&N (tr). 123
Alamy Images: Sergey Komarov-Kohl (crb). Courtesy of the National Science Foundation: Robyn Waserman (br)
Jacket images: Front: Alamy Images: Ashley Cooper / Global Warming Images cb; H. Mark Weidman Photography t. Dreamstime.com: Yury
Kuzmin / Polygraphus ca. Spine: Courtesy of the National Science Foundation: Robyn Waserman t. Back: Courtesy of the National Science
Foundation: Jack Green. Endpaper: Courtesy of the National Science Foundation: Dr. Paul Ponganis.
All other images © Dorling Kindersley
For further information see: www.dkimages.com

A WORLD OF IDEAS:
SEE ALL THERE IS TO KNOW

www.dk.com

CONTENTS

LOCATION

Antarctica is a vast land thousands of miles across, covered by an ice sheet thousands of feet deep. In the winter, Antarctica suffers the most hostile weather on Earth, with temperatures plummeting as low as -128°F (-89°C), and howling, hurricane-force winds. Aside from penguins, seals, and some other animals, only a few thousand scientists at research stations are brave enough to live in these harsh conditions.

W

AMUNDSEN
SEA

Key

 Ice sheet

 Permanent
sea ice

 Shoreline

Southern Ocean

4

0

SOUTHERN OCEAN

ANTARCTICA

South Pole

E

ROSS ICE
SHELF

Cape
Evans

McMurdo
Station

Ice-core
drilling station

GEORGE V
LAND

ROSS
SEA

Ninnis
Glacier

COMMONWEALTH BAY

Mertz
Glacier

Mawson's
hut

5

MEET THE TEAM

Scientists and explorers from around the world flock to Antarctica every year to conduct important research. Here is an example of some of the team members that you might find trekking through the snow and hiking over the ice.

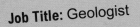 **Job Title:** Geologist

Description: studies rocks and metals and events such as earthquakes, floods, and volcanic eruptions.

Job Title: Mountaineering expert

Description: an expert climber who keeps the team safe on expeditions.

Job Title: Paleontologist

Description: studies fossils and whal they can tell us about the past.

Job Title: Biologist

Description: studies living organisms and how they interact with one another and adapt to changes in their environment.

Job Title: Meteorologist

Description: studies the atmosphere and researches weather patterns and climate change.

CHAPTER 1

At the southernmost point of the planet, there lies a land where the snowy landscape reaches as far as the horizon and blue-white icebergs litter the sea. This place is called Antarctica. Covering nine percent of the Earth's land, Antarctica is a vast and icy area. Largely untouched by humans, Antarctica has been the destination of choice for many explorers, as far back as the early 1800s. Today, the **continent** is populated with scientists and growing numbers of tourists.

Despite its chilly temperature, Antarctica is actually the world's largest desert. This is because it averages less than seven inches of

precipitation per year. Most precipitation on the continent falls as snow rather than rain because the temperatures are so low.

Antarctica is covered in a layer of ice, which in some areas is 7,000 ft (2,134 m) thick. However, this ice was not always there. It is thought that around 70 million years ago the area was semitropical. This means that the land would have been covered with deep forests and the surrounding sea would have been filled with dinosaurs and other giant reptiles.

Today, Antarctica is the coldest, windiest, and driest continent on the planet and only certain, well-adapted animals can survive there.

The coldest temperature that has ever been recorded on the surface of the Earth was taken at an Antarctic research station in 1983 and was a bitter -128.56°F (-89.2°C). These icy temperatures mean that it is easiest for humans to visit the continent during the summer months, which fall between December and February each year. The winter months bring brutal blizzards and darkness that continues for months at a time. This makes conditions very dangerous. The summer months bring the temperatures up to a slightly warmer 32°F (0°C). On mild days, temperatures may even jump up to a little warmer than freezing point. The sun often shines in Antarctica, but it still has the coldest summers on Earth!

There are many research stations in Antarctica that are occupied by scientists and support workers. In order to get to Antarctica, visitors have to travel by plane or boat. The planes that fly there have special modifications to ensure that they can land safely. Pegasus runway, which is located on the Ross Ice Shelf, is made of solid ice and is a safe place for planes to land. Other runways in Antarctica are more dangerous and only planes with skis are able to land on them.

Those who do spend time working and living in Antarctica have a range of special equipment available to them. Just as animals have had to **adapt** and evolve to survive the cold conditions, humans have also had to adapt their technology.

In the early days of Antarctic exploration, packs of dogs were used to pull sleds and carry explorers and their equipment across the icy plains. Nowadays, scientists and adventurers have faster modes of transportation. Snowmobiles are used instead of dogs to speed people to and from their work stations and tow heavy equipment behind them. Snowmobiles are essential because dogs are no longer allowed in Antarctica. People believed that they were spreading diseases to the seals.

For people who would like to investigate the polar regions there is the option of flying across the continent. Twin Otter planes are known as the workhorses of Antarctica because they travel up and down the continent, carrying people and equipment. With the ability to take off and land on short runways, and with special skis attached to them, they can land anywhere that there is a flat area of snow.

The southern continent of Antarctica is a frozen land surrounded by a blisteringly cold ocean. Its polar opposite is the Arctic, which is a frozen ocean surrounded by land. There are many different types of animals that live in the polar regions and these differ from the north to the south.

Ornithologists (scientists who study birds) travel to Antarctica in order to study the penguins and other birds that live there. Penguins are only found on the southern half of the planet and so do not live in the Arctic.

In contrast, polar bears are only found in the Arctic. This is lucky for the penguins. If the two animals shared a habitat, the penguins may well end up as a polar bear's dinner feast!

The Southern Ocean is brimming with whales, seals, and fish, which all play a very important part in the Antarctic marine ecosystem. Many of these sea creatures were previously threatened because humans were overfishing the southern waters. Some Antarctic species are now protected to ensure that the presence and actions of humans does not reduce their numbers even further. Some Antarctic fisheries are now the most heavily policed on the planet.

The Antarctic is a **treacherous** place for animals and humans alike. The ice that covers the land is the largest mass of ice on Earth and holds approximately 70 percent of the world's fresh water. Although it is not easy to see with the naked eye, this ice sheet is always on the move. This movement causes the ice to be pulled in many different directions, tearing it apart and creating cracks. These cracks form crevasses, which are deep chasms that are very dangerous and difficult to cross.

The movement of the ice also forms glaciers, which are huge ice rivers. These are pulled toward the ocean and eventually come to rest on top of the water, forming floating ice blocks called ice shelves. Occasionally, chunks will break away from the shelf and float off into the ocean—these are called icebergs and can be very dangerous for passing ships.

During the winter months the ocean surrounding Antarctica freezes and causes it to almost double in size. In summer, this ice melts, reducing it back down to a mass that is roughly 1.5 times as big as the United States.

ANTARCTIC WEATHER

The days continue to be long and sunny this summer for most of Antarctica. We're seeing an unusual amount of precipitation in some areas, though, with snow over the Ross Ice Shelf and around George V Land.

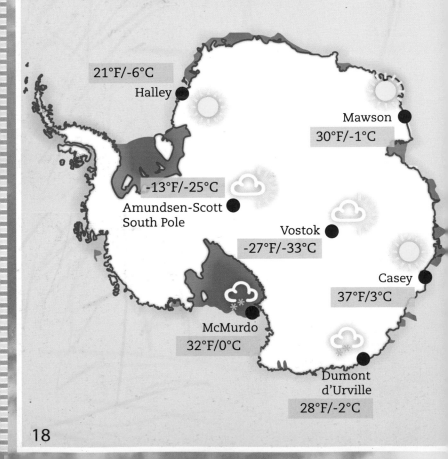

Summer Temperatures

21°F/-6°C
Halley

Mawson
30°F/-1°C

-13°F/-25°C
Amundsen-Scott
South Pole

Vostok
-27°F/-33°C

Casey
37°F/3°C

McMurdo
32°F/0°C

Dumont
d'Urville
28°F/-2°C

McMurdo Forecast

JANUARY 15

HIGH 36°F/2°C
LOW 28°F/-2°C

Chance of precipitation	70%
Wind	NW at 10 to 20 mph/16 to 32 kph
Humidity	0.03%
Sunrise	Up all day
Sunset	Up all day

Thurs	Fri	Sat	Sun
HIGH 34°F/1°C LOW 28°F/-2°C	HIGH 39°F/4°C LOW 28°F/-2°C	HIGH 32°F/0°C LOW 21°F/-6°C	HIGH 25°F/-4°C LOW 21°F/-6°C

Around Antarctica

Amundsen-Scott South Pole	HIGH -11°F/-24°C LOW -17°F/-27°C
Casey	HIGH 41°F/5°C LOW 32°F/0°C
Dumont d'Urville	HIGH 32°F/0°C LOW 27°F/-3°C
Halley	HIGH 34°F/1°C LOW 10°F/-12°C
Mawson	HIGH 34°F/1°C LOW 27°F/-3°C
Vostok	HIGH -17°F/-27°C LOW -38°F/-39°C

THE SNOW SPORTS CATALOGUE

Travel around the Antarctic in comfort and style with our state-of-the-art transportation devices. Don't let the harsh and treacherous conditions get the better of you! Let us help keep you safe and sound.

TWIN OTTER PLANE

Ensure safe transportation of yourself and your equipment by traveling in the Twin Otter aircraft. This high-wing, twin-engine plane has been designed with remote and dangerous environments in mind, making it strong and reliable in even the harshest of weather conditions. The Twin Otter is well-equipped with both wheels and skis, enabling it to take off safely and land anywhere, from a concrete runway to an icy glacier. With a maximum speed of 180 mph (290 kph), the Twin Otter will get you where you want to be faster than you can say "penguin!"

SNOWMOBILE XT80

This land vehicle provides explorers with a speedy and fun way of zipping around the Antarctic landscape. Getting you close to nature, this vehicle provides a safe and exciting way for you to experience the snowy continent. It has the ability to move at speeds of up to 70 mph (112 kph) and features that provide a smooth ride, allowing it to move over unstable ground with ease. The skis at the front of the vehicle provide you with superb directional control and precision when navigating over snow and ice.

FROSTNIP CROSS-COUNTRY SKIS

Frostnip cross-country skis are the premier products for the modern, intrepid explorer. Expertly crafted and using the latest in snow-travel technology, these skis are a must-have for any adventurer. The core of the skis is made from a dense maple wood, with tips made of a lighter aspen. This makes the skis lightweight, so maneuvering on ice and snow is easy. These skis are strong and durable to make sure that skiers can cross the toughest terrain.

21

GROUND-TO-AIR SIGNALS

If you get stuck out in the middle of Antarctica, you'll need to find ways to communicate with planes and helicopters overhead. Here are some ground signals you can use.

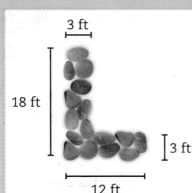

3 ft

18 ft

3 ft

12 ft

Letter height:
3 ft (1 m) wide by
18 ft (5.5 m) high

Letter width:
12 ft (3.5 m) wide
by 3 ft (1 m) high

Require doctor—
serious injuries

Aircraft badly
damaged

Require medical
supplies

Will attempt
to take off

Not understood

Require engineer

Unable to proceed

Probably safe
to land here

Require food
and water

Indicate direction
to proceed

Am going in
this direction

All well

Require food
and oil

No—negative

Require compass
and map

Require signal
lamp

Yes—affirmative

CHAPTER 2

Brave explorers and fearless scientists venture to the frozen south in the hope of finding the secrets of our planet underneath the ice. There are numerous research bases spread over the snowy scenery, each one hoping to unearth something new and exciting.

Scientists take readings from the ice, atmosphere, and ocean in order to understand how our planet works and to what extent human pollution is affecting it.

The largest research station in Antarctica is called McMurdo, and it is the home to the United States Antarctic Program. One of the major projects that the team at McMurdo undertakes is ice core drilling. By doing this, scientists can look to the past in the hope of finding information about the future.

Ice cores are long tubes of ice that have been drilled out of an ice sheet. In order for scientists to find a thick piece of ice to drill into, they need to leave the safety of McMurdo base camp and venture out into the wilderness. Scientists will often have to live and work on the ice for up to six weeks while they are drilling and examining ice cores.

Before starting their journey, scientists first send a Twin Otter plane out to their planned drilling site. The plane will scout out a safe place to land and will make one journey with tents, stoves, and enough fuel and food for a couple of weeks, as well as lots of survival gear. This is an important precaution that will protect the team if a blizzard hits and the next flight carrying equipment is delayed. This way the team will have everything they need to survive until the weather improves.

The first job once they are at their new campsite is to set up the radio communications.

If the team can't make contact with McMurdo the pilots will have to take them back. Being out of touch with the base is far too dangerous—help should always be close at hand.

Once the team has set up their camp, they need to construct the ice core drilling tent. This means digging out a trench about 7 ft (2 m) deep and 10 ft (3 m) wide for the ice core drill to stand in. This can be incredibly hard work because the air is very thin.

The top of the Antarctic ice is situated high above sea level and so there is less oxygen to breathe than down at McMurdo. The center of the ice sheet is about 13,000 ft (3,962 m) above sea level, which is almost as high as 10 Empire State Buildings! At this height people often suffer from altitude sickness, which can cause headaches and exhaustion. Most people **acclimatize** to the height, but some have to return to sea level to make them feel better.

Once the tent and equipment have been set up, the team will be ready to get drilling and start examining the ice cores that they find.

In order to extract the ice, the scientists have to use an auger. This is a seven-foot long metal tube with sharp teeth at one end. The auger cuts down through the ice, making an ice core. When it is full it is pulled up and the ice is taken out. Then it is dropped back down, ready to dig deeper.

The ice cores have air bubbles in them, which tell scientists about what the Earth was like in the past. The Antarctic ice sheet is made of snow that has fallen over hundreds of thousands of years. Ice that's 1,000 ft (305 m) down fell about 10,000 years ago.

As layers of snow build up on the land, they become squashed down to form ice. The air bubbles trapped inside tell scientists what types of gases were in the air at the time the ice was formed. This helps them to figure out how the **climate** is changing and what to expect for the future.

Scientists also look for layers of volcanic ash in the ice. If they find a layer of ash, it shows that a volcano erupted—if the ash is thick enough to see, it is evidence of a major eruption. Mount Erebus is the second highest of Antarctica's volcanoes and is still active. An active volcano is one that could erupt at any time, causing more ash to fall onto the ice. Sometimes the ash layer is too small to see with the naked eye so the ice core specimens are labeled and sent to a laboratory for further analysis.

Life out at the drilling camp is often difficult and dangerous and storms are likely to blow over the tents at any moment. Back at McMurdo base camp, however, the daily routine is much easier to adapt to. With many custom-built structures, McMurdo offers its visitors calming home comforts in the coldest corner of the world.

At McMurdo, as well as the living spaces and canteen, there are: laboratories, a firehouse, a power plant, stores, and clubs all linked by water, telephone, and power lines.

McMurdo also has tons of support workers—they're the folks who keep the whole place running! McMurdo has computer technicians, electricians, carpenters, cooks, janitors, pilots, mechanics…the list goes on! It just goes to show that it's not only scientists and tourists who are able to experience the wonders of the Antarctic continent.

Often, workers are trapped at their bases for days at a time due to bad weather. Weather conditions are numbered from 1–3. A three means normal weather and a one means very dangerous weather, when the temperatures drop to -100°F (-73°C) and the wind picks up to a speedy 200 mph (320 km/h).

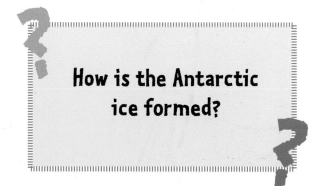

How is the Antarctic ice formed?

Another reason that scientists will have to leave the safety of their base camp is to set up Global Positioning System (GPS) stations. These are essential in drawing up maps of the area, which prevent people from getting lost in the Antarctic wilderness. Finding your way around such a vast, blank landscape is often a very tricky task because the snow reaches as far as the eye can see. There are very few landmarks to use as guides.

GPS is a satellite-based navigation system that relies upon 24 satellites, which are 12,000 miles (19,312 km) above the Earth. These satellites are constantly moving and circle the Earth twice a day at speeds of up to 7,000 mph (11,265 km/h). The receivers must pick up the signal of at least three different satellites in order to calculate an accurate position. These readings, combined with photographs taken from the air, help scientists to map out the great snowy expanse.

Ice in the Antarctic ice sheet is always moving. It forms in a slight dome shape as gravity pulls the underlying ice down the slope and toward the sea. GPS receivers placed out on the ice automatically radio their position to base camp every day. The receiver's position is measured once a day and its location is calculated to the nearest centimeter—that's around half an inch. The GPS used in Antarctica is a hundred times more accurate than the GPS in your phone or your car, so there is no chance of error. By using this method, scientists can monitor how fast and far the ice and glaciers are moving.

WHAT TYPE OF POLAR EXPLORER ARE YOU?

In order for an Antarctic expedition to work, it needs people with lots of different interests and skills to work together. Choose the activity that you enjoy most from each of the groups below. Then add up your answers to find out what type of polar explorer you are.

GROUP 1
A. Figuring out how something works
B. Drawing, painting, or taking photos
C. Being in a club
D. Being neat and tidy
E. Being a leader
F. Fixing things

GROUP 2
A. Working with electronics
B. Playing music or singing
C. Going to a party
D. Being organized
E. Negotiating with someone
F. Building things

GROUP 3
A. Watching science fiction movies
B. Dancing
C. Giving advice
D. Keeping records
E. Selling things
F. Playing sports

GROUP 4

A. Solving math problems
B. Writing
C. Explaining things to people
D. Following rules
E. Arguing your point of view
F. Using tools

YOUR ANTARCTIC CAREER PATH

Mostly As: Climatologist
You enjoy trying to figure out how the world works and are good at completing tasks on your own.

Mostly Bs: Photographer
You like trying new things and enjoy looking at and creating beautiful scenes and objects.

Mostly Cs: Psychologist
You get along well with others and are good at understanding their feelings.

Mostly Ds: Deputy team leader
You're a fantastic organizer and planner and like neatness and tidiness.

Mostly Es: Team leader
You like being in charge and are good at influencing others.

Mostly Fs: Radio operator
You enjoy working with machines and fixing things.

BASE OF OPERATIONS

Welcome to McMurdo Station! Here you will have everything you need during your stay in Antarctica. Take a look around!

KEY:

A Vehicle Maintenance Facility (VMF) takes care of polar vehicles
B Movement Control Center (MCC) manages cargo shipments
C Dormitories
D Building 155 houses the cafeteria, offices, and the store
E Medical center
F Fire station
G Science Support Center (SSC) looks after machinery used in scientific research
H Crary Science and Engineering Center is a research facility
I Chalet houses offices and meeting rooms
J Helicopter landing pad
K Power plant
L Water plant
M Waste water treatment plant

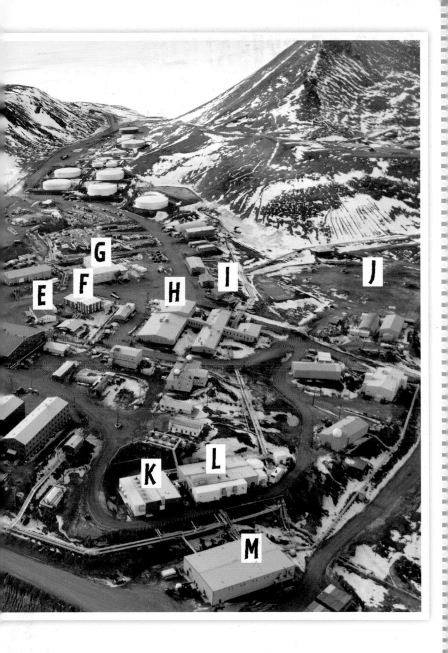

FACT FILE | ICE-CORE DRILLING

Since Antarctica remains icy throughout the year, snow that falls does not melt away and disappear. Instead, it builds up over thousands of years and forms solid ice. This ice can provide many clues about what the climate was like thousands of years ago.

Firn
The top layer consists of firn, which is snow that has partially melted, refrozen, and become dense from the pressure of the snow above it. It takes about two years to form.

Readings taken from Vostok Station

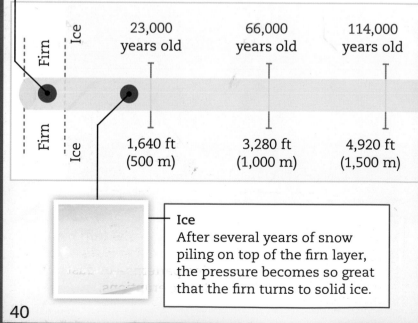

Firn	Ice	23,000 years old	66,000 years old	114,000 years old
Firn	Ice	1,640 ft (500 m)	3,280 ft (1,000 m)	4,920 ft (1,500 m)

Ice
After several years of snow piling on top of the firn layer, the pressure becomes so great that the firn turns to solid ice.

ICE CORES AND CLIMATE CHANGE

By examining which elements were in the air and in what quantities they existed, scientists can determine how warm the Earth was in the past. They can then figure out whether the Earth is getting warmer. By studying climate-change patterns, they can also predict how the climate might change in the future.

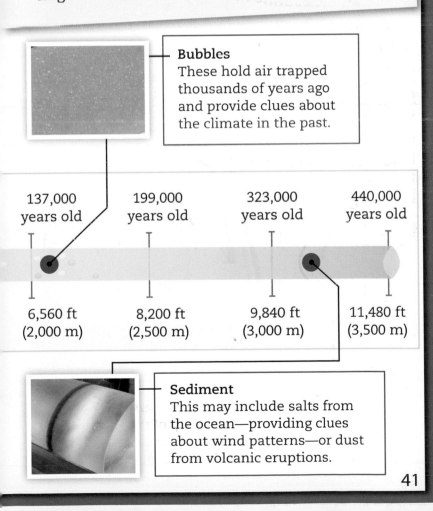

Bubbles
These hold air trapped thousands of years ago and provide clues about the climate in the past.

137,000 years old	199,000 years old	323,000 years old	440,000 years old
6,560 ft (2,000 m)	8,200 ft (2,500 m)	9,840 ft (3,000 m)	11,480 ft (3,500 m)

Sediment
This may include salts from the ocean—providing clues about wind patterns—or dust from volcanic eruptions.

41

CHAPTER 3

Survival is difficult in the unforgiving Antarctic environment. New recruits have to undergo a **rigorous** training program to make sure they are ready to tackle anything the continent has to throw at them.

Antarctic weather can be harsh, even in summer. The temperature can drop to a bone-chilling -20°F (-29°C), and there are often blizzards and gale-force winds called katabatics. This sort of weather is life threatening.

Crevasses, or deep cracks in the ice, are another major hazard. Anyone who is heading for a remote field station must be on the lookout for them in order to survive.

In an emergency, it might take days for help to arrive. One of the first lessons to learn is first aid. Recruits must learn how to identify and treat conditions that are common in Antarctica; these include hypothermia, frostbite, and snow blindness.

Next, they are taught how to dress properly. Wearing layers of clothes stops body heat from escaping and gloves, boots, and face masks are vital to prevent frostbite. Ski goggles are used to prevent snow blindness. There is certainly a lot to remember!

Next the trainees must learn how to set up a campsite—choosing a safe area is vital. A flat area is best so that the tent doesn't slide downhill in the middle of the night. It is also best to avoid areas with powdery snow. This means that wind has blown snow here recently so the tent may soon be buried.

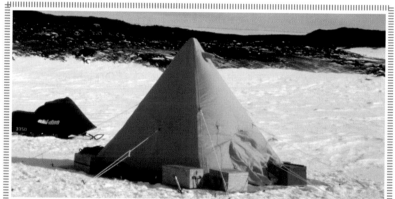

Modern explorers use pyramid tents, which are square at the base and pointed at the top. These are very stable and snow is often piled around the base of the tent to keep out the biting wind.

If explorers are ever stranded without equipment they can also build igloos for shelter. Believe it or not, an igloo is actually warmer than a tent, even though it's made of ice. However, it does take a long time to build. Digging a snow cave is better if shelter is required quickly. A snow cave is a shelter that consists of a long, narrow hole that is dug out of a snow drift or mound. Snow caves provide warmth and shelter and explorers have even been known to survive terrifying storms by hiding out in them.

For scientists and explorers who brave the dangerous and barren world of Antarctica, staying in contact with base camp is crucial. If the team finds themselves in trouble (and there are many things in Antarctica that can cause perilous problems!) they will have to radio for help.

However, prevention is better than cure, and trying to stay out of harm's way is always the best option. Knowing how to **navigate** from one place to the other in such a white and sparse area is very difficult, but doing so keeps explorers in safer territory. This can be a big challenge and is a skill that new recruits have to learn. Modern explorers will use GPS units, maps, and magnetic compasses to cross the ice.

Navigation without GPS is very tricky in Antarctica because explorers can travel for hundreds of miles without seeing any landmarks. Compasses will also not work properly if they are too close to the south pole. The south end of a compass needle always points to the South Magnetic Pole. If explorers pass too close to the pole then the needle will swing around to point in a different direction. This can be very disorienting!

One perilous pitfall that GPS systems and compasses can't guard against are crevasses. These can open up anytime and anywhere on the Antarctic ice and falling into one is a terrifying and potentially deadly accident.

Crevasses are well hidden below thin bridges of snow, making them almost invisible. These snow bridges are deceptive and are usually only a few inches thick. They are not strong enough to hold a human, and if you step on one you are likely to be plunged into the icy depths below.

These troublesome gaps can endanger even the most seasoned mountaineer and even though risks can be minimized by using proper safety measures, they can never be completely eliminated.

The safest way for explorers to travel across treacherous areas is to use rope-travel techniques. This is when explorers tie themselves and their snowmobiles together using long lengths of rope. This way, if someone does happen to slip into the dark pit of a crevasse, the rope should stop them from falling all the way to the bottom. If roped up correctly the victim should just dangle in midair and the other members of their expedition team will be able to use the rope to hoist them out again.

Being careful when traveling through areas that are likely to have crevasses is the kind of thing that could save your life when in Antarctica. All teams that venture out into the isolated ice land will have a field guide with them. This will be an expert who knows the tricks of the trade when it comes to working in the snow. Sometimes teams will be working so far away from their base that it could take an aircraft over four hours to reach them.

Whiteouts are another common problem that teams will experience in Antarctica. This is when the snow is picked up by the wind and blankets the area in a thick sea of white. The deep mist makes it very difficult to see where the land stops and the sky begins. It is almost impossible for anyone to move around safely. Even moving just a few feet can be extremely perilous.

This fog can cause people to become disoriented. The best way to ride out a whiteout is to sit tight inside a tent. It is not safe for anyone to try and move until the storm has completely blown over and the environment is back to its smooth, gleaming landscape.

Hiking across the snow is physically and mentally demanding work. Having a supportive team around you helps to keep spirits up and morale high. Even though Antarctica can appear to be scarily vast, there are times when the snow gleams and the ice sparkles in the sun. This incredible and uplifting sight has inspired explorers, artists, musicians, and filmmakers for years, and many who are privileged enough to witness it, know that it is a once-in-a-lifetime opportunity.

Antarctica is filled with sights and sounds that humans are not able to experience in many other places on the Earth. Rarely will anyone get to feel such bone-chilling temperatures or look out over a land that is so serene and calm. The creaking of the ice underfoot is often punctuated by the thunderous roar and splash of an iceberg breaking away from a glacier. These sights, sounds, and experiences can be breathtaking and terrifying all at once and are just a few of the reasons why people need to work hard to preserve this impressive terrain for generations to come.

GLACIERS AND ICEBERGS

A glacier is a huge, slow-moving river of ice. Icebergs form when huge chunks of ice from glaciers break off and fall into the ocean.

GLACIER ANATOMY

Cirque:
deep recess in a mountain with steep walls.

Icefall:
glacier flows over a steep slope.

Rockfall:
fragments of loosened rock that fall from the face of a cliff.

Crevasse:
deep crack in a glacier caused by motion.

Rock avalanche:
when ground movement causes rocks to fall.

Englacial debris:
rocks that are carried along with a glacier.

ICEBERG SHAPES

Tabular:
steep sides with
a flat top, like
a huge tablet.

Blocky:
box-shaped,
with steep,
vertical sides.

Wedge:
top narrowing
to a pyramid-
like point.

Pinnacle:
having one or
more spires
rising very high.

Arch:
arched opening in
the middle due
to erosion.

Dome:
very rounded
and smooth top.

Lateral moraine:
pile of rocks that forms
alongside the glacier.

Glacial lake:
lake formed by
a melting glacier.

Terminal moraine:
rock pieces that form at
the end of a glacier.

Outwash plain:
sand, gravel, and mud that have
washed out from a glacier.

55

HOW TO BUILD AN IGLOO

YOU WILL NEED

- waterproof gloves
- warm clothes
- shovel
- large serrated kitchen knife
- old woodworking saw
- lots of snow

KNIVES ARE SHARP!
GET AN ADULT TO HELP YOU.

1 Find some hard-packed snow and ask an adult to use the saw or knife to cut some large rectangular blocks. Stand the blocks in a circle and cut the tops so that they slope down toward the center.

2 Use the shovel to dig out about 3 ft (1 m) of snow from the inside of the circle. Leave a section at the back of the igloo to make a seat.

3 Cut more blocks with slanted tops and place them on top of the first layer across the joints between the blocks below.

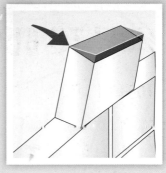

4 When the wall is high enough, cut an arched doorway into one side of the igloo and dig an entrance passageway. Build a tunnel over the entranceway.

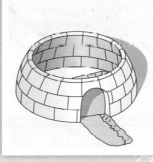

5 Add more layers to the igloo, with each one leaning farther in to form the dome.

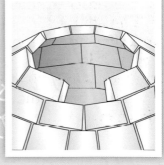

6 Plug any gaps with snow, but make sure to leave small holes in the roof to let in fresh air. Your igloo is now finished.

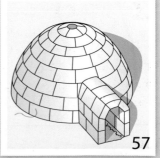

ANTARCTIC AILMENTS

Good morning. Welcome to the McMurdo Medical Center. Our team specializes in the many diseases and ailments that occur in the harsh Antarctic conditions. We will do our best to treat you as soon as possible. Please take a seat, and someone will see you shortly.

Patient 1
Date: January 25

History: patient has been working with the ice-drilling team and has been forced to work long shifts for the past two weeks. No previous medical problems or allergies.

Examination: patient has complained that he has trouble concentrating and staying awake during the day. Patient has also experienced hallucinations.

Diagnosis: sleep deprivation.

Treatment: take some time off work and try to get eight hours of uninterrupted sleep each night. Eat healthily and drink plenty of fluids.

Patient 2
Date: July 1

History: family history of diabetes.

Examination: patient is shivering violently and is having trouble breathing. Her skin is very pale and her temperature reading shows 93.2°F (34°C). Normal body temperature should be around 98.6°F (37°C).

Diagnosis: hypothermia.

Treatment: patient is to remove wet clothing and be wrapped in warm towels and blankets. Patient is to be given a warm drink and some high-energy food.

Patient 3
Date: August 2

History: patient was lost outside in a snow blizzard for a number of hours.

Examination: patient is experiencing a tingling sensation in his fingers, which are also throbbing and aching. His skin feels very cold and looks white.

Diagnosis: frostnip—not as severe as frostbite.

Treatment: patient has been advised to warm his hands slowly by placing them in warm (but not hot) water. His fingers should then be wrapped in bandages to avoid infection.

CHAPTER 4

During the great Age of Discovery, explorers crisscrossed the globe. They found and mapped many new places, but the southernmost part of the Earth remained an unexplored mystery. Some people thought there was only water there, whereas others believed there to be a huge land mass, but no one knew for sure. In 1772, British explorer, James Cook, set off on a three-year voyage to sail as far south as possible, and find the truth.

Cook's journey was a dangerous one. The seas were stormy and filled with massive icebergs, and the wind and rain battered his boat. Cook never reached Antarctica because of the icy walls surrounding it. He had found no mega-continent, but believed there must be land at the South Pole.

Since Cook's expedition, many teams of brave explorers have set out to map the uncharted southern territory, determined to find, study, and explore the unknown land.

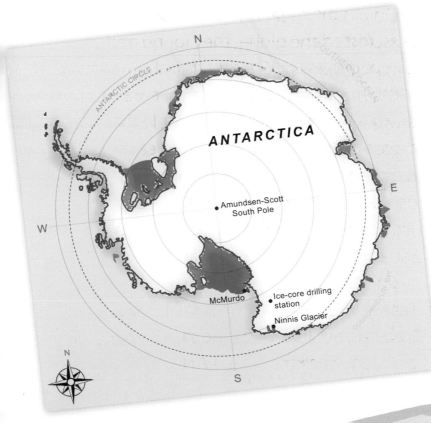

Over the decades, many explorers have gone in search of the South Pole and the glory and honor that goes with reaching it. However, there are also many scientists who have braved the churning seas and the bitter cold, just to study the glaciers, rocks, and wildlife there.

One such man was Douglas Mawson. His expedition, which started in 1911, is one of the most shocking survival stories of all time.

Mawson first came to Antarctica with Ernest Shackleton in 1907. On that expedition, the team traveled more than 1,000 miles (about 1,600 km) over the ice sheet in the hope of reaching the pole. Amazingly, they hauled their own sleds all the way but sadly did not complete their mission.

Inspired by his expedition with Shackleton, Mawson organized his own trip to the south in 1911—the Australasian Antarctic Expedition. His men built a hut at Commonwealth Bay to live and work in and for three years Mawson studied the rocks, the glaciers, the wildlife, and the weather.

One day Mawson set out from his base to make detailed maps of Antarctica. He took two men with him—Belgrave Ninnis and Xavier Mertz. Little did they know that this expedition would change their lives forever.

Douglas Mawson 1882–1958
Australian geologist and Antarctic explorer

Thirty five days into the expedition the men found themselves in a rather tragic situation. Ninnis had misjudged a crevasse and had fallen straight into it, taking his sled and dog team with him. Looking over the edge of the crevasse, all that Mertz and Mawson were able to see was an injured dog, lying on a shelf about 150 ft (46 m) down. Ninnis and his sled had disappeared.

Mawson and Mertz tried with all their might to save Ninnis from certain death in the crevasse, but sadly they did not succeed. They had to leave Ninnis behind. This is why that particular part of Antarctica is now called the Ninnis Glacier.

Mawson and Mertz were forced to continue as a pair but they did not have enough food to last them. Most of their food and their dog's food had been tied to Ninnis's sled and had been swept away into the gloomy darkness when he fell. Mawson and Mertz were weeks away from base and were in desperate trouble.

With nothing to eat, the men and their dogs were becoming weaker and weaker, and one by one their dogs started to die.

Mawson and Mertz were so short on food that they had to resort to drastic measures— eating their dogs in order to stay alive. This kept them going for a while but with no dogs left, they had to pull their sleds themselves and gradually they also grew sickly and sluggish.

The men threw away their heavy equipment to make their sleds lighter. This even included Mawson's precious camera and films. Mertz became very sick and got badly frostbitten. In the end he couldn't continue.

Mawson soldiered on, putting Mertz on his sled and trying to pull him to safety. Eventually however, Mertz died and Mawson was forced to bury him in the snow.

Mawson was exhausted and felt very sick, but he kept going alone. In a desperate attempt to make his journey easier, Mawson cut his sled in half to make it lighter and easier to pull. Astonishingly, he managed to do this with just the small pocketknife that he had with him.

With hope quickly fading, Mawson struggled through the snow in the direction of his hut and the prospect of survival.

27c

AUSTRALIAN
ANTARCTIC
TERRITORY

Sir Douglas Mawson Centenary—1982

Mawson began to think that even if he did make it back to his hut alive, his ship, the *Aurora*, and all his men, would have left. Winter was starting to close in on the continent.

As if he had not already had enough bad luck, in his dazed and tired state, Mawson stumbled into a crevasse, just like his friend Ninnis. Mawson was left dangling on a rope, and had to use all the energy he could muster to pull himself out again. With incredible willpower he managed to scramble over the edge of the crevasse, onto the cold, slippery ice above.

Mawson continued for 20 more days and just when he thought he could not go any farther, he found a stash of food. What a miracle! It had been left for him by a search party from his base. That food saved his life.

It was only another 25 miles (40 km) to the hut, but it took Mawson ten long days to get there. When Mawson reached the hut he was distraught to discover that his ship had left only five hours before he arrived. However, a small team of men had stayed behind in case he did return. What relief he must have felt!

So, after all his trials, Mawson was safe and he returned home with his crew. This was one of the most incredible feats of survival in the history of the Antarctic.

The Antarctic environment can push people to their very limits and challenge even the most courageous explorers. One amazing feat of endurance that took place on the Antarctic ice was the great race to the pole in 1911. The two competitors were Norwegian adventurer Roald Amundsen and British Royal Navy officer, Captain Robert Falcon Scott. The two men and their teams fought long and hard to be crowned the first man to reach the South Pole, but in the end there could only be one winner.

Roald Amundsen was a seasoned explorer who had already won fame for being the first to sail the Arctic's Northwest Passage. He was a well-organized and practical man. He also knew the best way to tackle the difficult and often treacherous Antarctic terrain.

Captain Scott made his first voyage to Antarctica in 1901, during which his team built a hut in order to conduct scientific research. His team also made an attempt to travel farther south than anyone had before them, but was woefully unprepared and had to turn back after they experienced health problems caused by poor nutrition. On his second trip to the south, Scott and his team set out with renewed determination and an aim to reach the South Pole. The race was on.

The two expedition teams had different levels of skill when it came to trekking through the snow. Amundsen and his team were experienced skiiers and dog drivers, and their main goal was to reach the pole as quickly as possible. They took 52 dogs with them to pull their sleds of food and equipment. As the sleds became lighter, Amundsen killed his dogs to feed his men.

Scott's team, on the other hand, had a rather more disastrous time. Knowing little about the use of dogs or skis, Scott's team tried to pull their sleds themselves, which was backbreaking work. The men had to survive on a diet of tasteless crackers and pemmican, which was a combination of ground meat and melted fat.

Needless to say, Amundsen and his team were the victors—reaching the pole just over one month before Scott. With heavy hearts, Scott's team turned around and began the journey back to their hut on Cape Evans. The team battled heroically through blizzards and gale-force winds. However, their bodies were quickly becoming weak and their food and fuel supplies were shrinking. It seemed as though the odds were stacked against Captain Scott and his team.

"BOVRIL" PEMMICAN.

A highly sustaining food, consisting of Albumen and Fibrine of Beef, and Animal Fat, etc. For use in cold regions.

BOVRIL, LIMITED, LONDON, E.C. 1.

The thought of the food and warmth that would greet them upon their return, spurred on Scott and his team, but sadly this was not enough to save them. The days were getting shorter and the temperature was dropping. The team was in grave danger.

The harsh conditions got the better of the men and, one by one, they died. Soon, just Captain Scott and three other men were left. One of the men, Lawrence Oates, had frostbite on his feet and knew that he could not go on. One fateful night he left the tent during a blizzard, announcing to his team, "I am just going outside, and I may be some time." Oates never returned. The last three men, including Scott himself, died in their tent not long after the disappearance of Oates. They were found only 11 miles (18 km) from reaching help.

A search party was sent out for Scott and his men. Their papers and journals were recovered but their bodies were left in their final resting places, under the snow.

Scott's hut on Cape Evans is still there today for modern explorers and tourists to visit. Many of the things inside have been preserved. The kitchen is full of food cans, books, and magazines, and clothes are still strewn around the hut, just as if the men might return from their expedition at any moment.

Since the early 1900s, there have been many more expeditions to the southern continent. Modern scientists and explorers have learned how to live and work in the cold conditions and, fortunately, the risk of **fatality** has been greatly reduced.

When Antarctic explorers and scientists set foot on the ice nowadays, they make sure that they are sufficiently dressed in the warmest, insulating clothes and footwear. In addition to staying snug, they also have a more varied array of food available to them. When working at a main station such as McMurdo, the meals will be very similar to those from home. The only difference is that fruit and vegetables are limited and come canned, dried, or frozen.

When scientists are working at remote field sites they are given ration boxes that are filled with high-calorie foods, providing them with a healthy and balanced diet. These boxes contain freeze-dried main meals, dried soup, dried vegetables, coffee, cookies, and chocolate.

Many are also given a "goodie" box, which includes luxury items such as herbs, spices, and even ketchup.

One thing that is in abundance in Antarctica is water in the form of ice. People can heat the ice and melt it into water that is safe to drink and use for cooking food.

Science, technology, and exploration have advanced in leaps and bounds in recent years, and these fields will always be fueled by human curiosity. During World War II, the British Government **deployed** a group of people to the Antarctic region to look for enemy activity. This led to permanent bases being built on the land, which signaled the start of the modern era of research on the continent.

Between 1949–1952 the first expedition to involve scientists from different countries was launched. The international group involved Norwegian, British, Canadian, Australian, and Swedish scientists who worked together to study the climate. Although the team made some important discoveries, the expedition was not without its problems. In 1951, bad weather caused one of the tractors to plunge over an ice cliff, killing three people.

In 1992 another great feat of endurance was undertaken by Dr. Mike Stroud and Ranulph Feinnes, who made an unsupported (not using any dogs or machines) crossing of Antarctica. Despite their heavy sleds, low blood sugar levels, and general poor health, the pair managed to walk a staggering 1,350 miles (2,173 km) in 95 days.

FAMOUS ANTARCTIC EXPLORERS

| Popular topics | Quizzes | Galleries | Lists |

Captain Robert Falcon Scott *(1868–1912)*

Captain Scott led two expeditions to Antarctica: the first was in 1901–1904 and the second was in 1910–1913. His second expedition aimed to reach the South Pole. Scott and his team reached the Pole on January 17, 1912, but, unfortunately, they were not the first people there. Scott and his team did not survive the journey home; they all died from the extreme cold and lack of food.

Sir Ernest Shackleton *(1874–1922)*

In 1901, Shackleton joined Captain Robert Falcon Scott's unsuccessful expedition to the South Pole. He then set out to reach the Pole again in 1906. His team didn't make it all the way there, but did get closer than anyone had before. Shackleton's most famous journey to Antarctica was in 1914 in *HMS Endurance*, his ship that was crushed by the ice.

Sir Douglas Mawson (1882–1958)

Douglas Mawson was a geologist who dedicated many years to uncovering the scientific secrets of Antarctica. In 1907, he joined Ernest Shackleton's Nimrod expedition and completed the longest man-hauling sled journey, which lasted 122 days. In 1911, Mawson led his own trip to Antarctica. His team got into trouble on the Ninnis Glacier, and Mawson was the only one to survive.

Roald Amundsen (1872–1928)

Roald Amundsen was the first explorer to reach the South Pole. His team reached the pole on December 14, 1911, just over one month before Captain Scott. Amundsen and his team were experienced skiers and dog drivers, so they were able to move much faster than Scott. Amundsen died in 1928, when his plane crashed while on a rescue mission in the Arctic.

81

ANTARCTIC APPAREL

Good evening, and welcome to our annual Antarctic Apparel Fashion Show. Our models will be displaying some of the best modern and retro clothing. Each item has been chosen by our expert panel to showcase designs from past and present that are not just chic, but also cozy.

CLASSIC CLOTHING

WOOLEN UNDERGARMENTS

Fashionable in the 1900s, woolen undergarments could be warm, but they had a major problem: when the wearer sweated, the clothing got wet and dried slowly. This left the wearer both cold and damp.

GLOVES

To keep out the cold, early Antarctic explorers would have worn woolen gloves topped with reindeer-fur mittens.

FINNESKO BOOTS

These boots would have been all the rage in the 1900s. Made from reindeer fur and with a lining of sennegrass (insulating grass), they would have kept explorers' feet warm and dry.

MODERN WINTER WEAR

THERMAL UNDERWEAR
Our model is sporting the latest designs in lightweight thermal underwear. This inner layer is worn next to the skin to help keep body heat in.

GOGGLES
These cool shades will protect your eyes from the glare of the sunlight reflecting off the snow.

OUTER LAYER
Turn heads in this eye-catching jacket. The goose-down core keeps you warm and toasty, while the nylon covering makes the outfit waterproof.

MITTENS
Your outfit wouldn't be complete without a stylish pair of mittens to keep your digits snug. This pair is double layered for warmth and has adjustable wrist straps to prevent snow from getting in.

GLACIER BOOTS
This pair of statement boots lets you step out in style. The thick, ridged rubber soles prevent you from slipping on any ice or snow.

MAWSON'S DIARY

The diary entry below includes a description of the disappearance of Ninnis. It is taken from Mawson's own account of the expedition, *Home of the Blizzard*, which was published in 1915.

December 14, 1912

A light east-south-east wind was blowing as the sleds started away eastward this morning. The weather was sunny, and the temperature registered 21 degrees F. Everything was, for once, in harmony, and the time was at hand when we should turn our faces homeward.

Mertz was well in advance of us when I noticed him hold up his ski stick and then go on. This was a signal for something unusual, so I looked out for crevasses or some other explanation of his action. On reaching the spot where Mertz had signaled and seeing no sign of any irregularity, I jumped on to the sled. Glancing at the ground a moment after, I noticed the faint indication of a crevasse. I turned quickly round, called out a warning word to Ninnis, and then dismissed it from my thoughts.

Then there was no sound from behind except a faint, plaintive whine from one of the dogs. When I next looked back, it was in response to the anxious gaze of Mertz, who had turned round and halted in his tracks. Behind me, nothing met the eye but my own sled tracks running back in the distance.

Where were Ninnis and his sled?

The lid of a crevasse had broken in; two sled tracks led up to it on the far side, but only one continued on the other side.

Lieutenant B.E.S. Ninnis, R.F.

I leaned over and shouted into the dark depths below. No sound came back but the moaning of a dog, caught on a shelf just visible one hundred and fifty feet below. Close by was what appeared in the gloom to be the remains of the tent and a canvas tank containing food for three men for a fortnight.

We broke back the edge of the névé (glacial snow) lid and took turns leaning over secured by a rope, calling into the darkness in the hope that our companion might still be alive. For three hours we called unceasingly, but no answering sound came back. We felt that there was little hope.

In such moments, action is the only tolerable thing. Stricken dumb with the pity of it and heavy at heart, we turned our minds mechanically to what lay nearest at hand.

85

RACE TO THE POLE!
AMUNDSEN VS. SCOTT

Departure from
base camp at the
Bay of Whales
October 20, 1911

486 miles (782 km)
to the Pole
November 9, 1911

AMUNDSEN

624 miles (1,005 km)
to the Pole
October 31, 1911

Arrival in the Antarctic
January 14, 1911

486 miles (782 km)
to the Pole
November 23, 1911

624 miles (1,005 km)
to the Pole
November 9, 1911

SCOTT

Arrival in the Antarctic
January 4, 1911

Departure from base
camp at Cape Evans
November 1, 1911

In 1911, two explorers—Robert Falcon Scott and Roald Amundsen—set out to attempt to be the first person to reach the South Pole. It was a fierce competition, but in the end, Amundsen won. Amundsen, a Norwegian, was an experienced polar traveler, having lived in the Arctic for several years. Many believe this was the secret of his success.

347 miles (558 km) to the Pole
November 17, 1911

112 miles (181 km) to the Pole
December 7, 1911

SOUTH POLE

347 miles (558 km) to the Pole
December 21, 1911

112 miles (181 km) to the Pole—the southernmost point reached by Ernest Shackleton in 1909
January 9, 1912

AMUNDSEN VS. SCOTT

1ST

Arrival at the Pole
December 14, 1911

2ND

Arrival at the Pole
January 17, 1912

THE MIDNIGHT SUN

Here are some examples of what explorers would have eaten in the early 1900s and what modern-day explorers would eat on expeditions nowadays.

◇ ◇ ◇ MENU ◇ ◇ ◇

The Midnight Sun is a brand-new café catering to the needs of Antarctic explorers. Our menu offers high-energy meals and snacks 24 hours a day.

BREAKFAST AND SNACKS

Pemmican (e)
Dried beef mixed with lard and berries

Whole-wheat crackers (e)
Served with butter

LUNCH AND DINNER

Hoosh (e)
Stew of whole-wheat crackers, pemmican, and snow

DRINKS

Tea
Hot cocoa
Both served with dried milk and sugar

DESSERT

Chocolate (e)
Bar of semisweet chocolate

e = high-energy food

MENU

It's been more than a hundred years, but the Midnight Sun is still providing polar explorers with all the high-energy food they need.

BREAKFAST AND SNACKS

Crackers (e)
Served with butter, cheese, peanut butter, or apricot jam

Dried-fruit salad (e)
With apples and apricots

Assorted nuts (e)

Granola or granola bars (e)
Served with dried milk powder mixed with water

DRINKS

Tea

Hot cocoa

Instant coffee

All served with dried milk and sugar

e = high-energy food

LUNCH AND DINNER

Noodle soup
Made from dried noodles and available in tomato and basil, chicken, or vegetable

Salmon (e)
Freeze dried and served with your choice of peas and carrots, peas and corn, or green beans

Ham (e)
From a can and served with potatoes and onions

Pasta (e)
With pesto, mushroom and bacon, or sour cream and chive sauce

Tuna (e)
Freeze dried and served with rice or noodles

DESSERT

Chocolate (e)
Dark, milk, or with peanuts

GHOSTS OF ANTARCTICA

There are many ghost stories about Antarctica. Some people say that it is the most haunted place on Earth. This is because it has more abandoned settlements than anywhere else. Would you want to visit any of these haunted places?

SCOTT'S HUT

Thanks to the cold, everything in Captain Scott's hut has been frozen in time, and items from the 1910s have been left exactly as they were. Scott and two others died on their way back to the hut in 1912. Since then, voices and footsteps have been heard in the cabin.

GRYTVIKEN

The Sub-Antarctic island of South Georgia was home to at least seven whaling communities at the beginning of the twentieth century. The most spectacular was Grytviken, which was founded in 1904. It is the final resting place of Ernest Shackleton but was abandoned in 1966. Its church remains as an eerie reminder of the thriving village it once was.

OUR LADY OF THE SNOWS

This shrine commemorates petty officer Richard T. Williams. He was killed on January 6, 1956, when the tractor he was driving broke through the ice off Cape Royds and fell to the bottom of McMurdo Sound. His body was never found, but Our Lady of the Snows was built in 1957 in his memory.

HEKTOR WHALING STATION

Deception Island is home to Hektor, one of the oldest ghost towns in Antarctica. It was built in 1912 as a whaling outpost. It was abandoned in 1931 and has been left untouched ever since. A cemetery and the tombs of thirty-five men were buried by a volcanic eruption in 1969.

THE TRUTH BEHIND THE TALES

Ghost sightings in Antarctica may actually be hallucinations. In the summertime in Antarctica, the sun never sets. This makes it difficult for some people to sleep, so they suffer from sleep deprivation (see p. 58), which causes hallucinations.

91

CHAPTER 5

Now that plucky explorers have risked their lives to chart the southern continent, the area is not as treacherous as it was years ago. It does, however, still hold many mysteries. Inexperienced explorers are able to visit the slice of ice and discover the wonders of the frozen continent for themselves.

Some airline companies run flights to the continent, but most tourists visit the icy land by boat. Cruise liners offer guests a five-star experience and give them the opportunity to enjoy the glaring white snow, shining icebergs, and extraordinary wildlife from the lap of luxury. Trips cost thousands of dollars but offer guests a unique experience of the big freezer.

Although lavish ships make polar travel more comfortable, they do not have a good effect on the Antarctic environment. Ships that travel to the area bring the danger of pollution with them—they carry so much fuel, that if they sink, the surrounding seas and inhabitants will be in grave danger. Tourists who set foot on the continent also need to be incredibly careful not to leave any garbage behind. The low temperatures freeze even **biodegradable** food waste, so it will remain frozen on the ice for decades afterward.

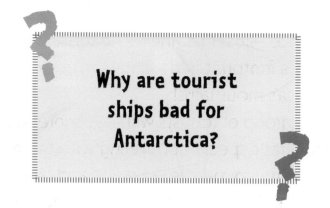

Why are tourist ships bad for Antarctica?

The first tourist ships set sail for Antarctica in the 1950s and since then the number of visitors has greatly increased. The numbers are now so high that rules have been put into place to minimize human impact on the surroundings.

All visitors have to comply with the Antarctic Treaty, do their best to protect the environment, and leave no trace on the continent. During their time on the ice, tourists can experience ice camping and also, for the more adventurous types, mountaineering. Not for the faint of heart, mountaineering is by no means easy, but can be a very rewarding experience—just imagine being the first person to make a footprint in the snow on one of Antarctica's mountains!

Every group of tourists will have more than one Antarctic specialist traveling with them, to guide them around the crevasses and over the mountains. These guides will also be able to give them some information about the area itself and the wonderful wildlife that live there.

The Antarctic animals are a great attraction for tourists and scientists alike. Scientists in Antarctica monitor the animals that live there: how many there are of each species, and how they breed, feed, and interact with one another. Penguins in particular are an incredible sight to behold.

The emperor penguin is the icon of Antarctica and in April every year, the continent is flooded with the waddling birds. Each penguin makes the pilgrimage to Antarctica in search of the perfect breeding ground. They will often have to travel up to 62 miles (100 km) across the ice in pitch darkness.

Once the female penguin has laid her egg the male will care for it. Then begins another amazing feat of endurance on the Antarctic ice. During the long winter months the male penguin will incubate the egg, which means that he will keep it warm, so that it can hatch. He will put the egg on his feet and nestle it under a flap of his warm, thick skin.

For two months, the male penguin cannot feed, or even move. He will therefore often lose around half of his body weight. During this time the female will leave on a long hunting trip and will only return once the chick has hatched.

Penguins are well-adapted to the subzero temperatures and have a thick layer of blubber and overlapping feathers to store as much heat as possible. Penguins are also intelligent creatures who will huddle close together in the winter months, in order to share their body heat with each other. The penguins in the center of the huddle are warmest and every so often will swap positions with the ones forming the outside barrier. This ensures that everyone gets a turn in the middle, protected from the cold, sharp wind.

Tourists and scientists go in search of all different creatures in the Antarctic. Some of the only animals that live on the land all year-round are tiny, often microscopic, creatures. All the other animals (including humans) are just visitors who spend most of their time on other continents or in the sea. An example of one such visitor is the seal.

Weddell seals that live in the Antarctic stay below the ice during the dark, winter months. Seals dive down to the depths of the ocean to catch fish to eat. Their sharp teeth and agile bodies enable them to gobble up fish with ease, and the Antarctic waters provide plenty so the seals will not go hungry.

Seals can dive to depths of 1,900 ft (580 m) and can stay under water for up to 70 minutes. Just imagine being able to hold your breath for that long! They chew on the ice to keep holes open so that they can pop up for some air whenever they are short of breath. Seals are among the hardiest of all polar animals and, like penguins, have a thick coat of blubber to keep them warm. In the summertime, when they become tired of the underwater life, they simply jump up onto the ice for a rest and a bit of sunbathing.

The Antarctic **ecosystem** is a well-balanced machine, and the **extinction** of one animal, no matter how small, can cause serious problems for others in the food web. Seals survive by eating the fish and squid from the Antarctic ocean, but they also provide food for some of the larger animals.

Seals are eaten by whales, who sometimes have to think creatively to catch their blubbery prey. The orcas, or killer whales, that live in Antarctica live in groups, or "pods," and will often work together to overpower seals to eat.

If a seal is caught off guard resting on an ice floe (piece of floating ice) by a pod of killer whales, it had better watch out! Killer whales are so strong and fast that they are able to swim together and create large waves. This will rock the ice floe and knock the seal into the water, where the whales are waiting to snap it up. This is a very cunning trick and demonstrates just how intelligent these sea mammals are.

Killer whales have sharp teeth for ripping meat off their prey, however whales such as the humpback whale have sievelike teeth called baleen. Baleen whales use these brush teeth to filter their food out of the water. Even though they are very large animals, they feed on small creatures, and their diet mainly consists of shrimplike critters called krill.

From the tiny to the titanic, Antarctica is a wonderland full of amazing animals, and is a fantastic place to observe creatures in their unspoiled, natural habitat.

Emperor penguins can "fly" out of the water to catch fish and hop up onto the ice.

PENGUIN PRISONER LINEUP

These pesky penguins have been stealing each other's pebbles!

These penguins are not as innocent as they look! They have all been caught red flippered and are being held under suspicion of theft and intimidation. Witnesses have reported that, in the dead of night, these penguins have been seen stealing stones and chicks from their unsuspecting neighbors. Let's hear the facts.

CHARGES

This penguin has been accused of stealing rocks from other penguins' nests. Witnesses have stated that they saw him taking the rocks and putting them in his own nest to help keep his egg warm until it hatched.

ADÉLIE PENGUIN
PRISONER: AP2556

FACT: Always planning their getaway, Adélie penguins can swim very fast. They can also jump more than 3 ft (1 m) out of the water and into the air, making them look as if they are flying.

CHARGES

This penguin is under suspicion of intimidation and theft. Not only has this thug been seen stealing stones, but he has also been spotted bullying the Adélie penguins out of their nesting site, hoping to make space for his own nest.

CHINSTRAP PENGUIN
PRISONER: CP6598

FACT: Chinstrap penguins are expert climbers. They use their beaks and claws to scale rocks and to find the perfect nesting sites.

CHARGES

This female penguin has been charged with kidnapping. After discovering that her baby chick was missing, she was so upset that she stole a chick from a neighboring penguin couple.

EMPEROR PENGUIN
PRISONER: EP1489

FACT: Instead of making nests, a male emperor penguin will rest his egg on his feet and cover it with a fold of skin to keep it warm. He stands like this for up to two months, and doesn't even move to eat.

CHAPTER 6

Antarctica is the last great wilderness left on Earth and humans need to try and keep it that way. The unfortunate thing is, humans are the ones who cause the most problems!

Seeing tourist ships glide around the Antarctic ice would have been unthinkable in the past. However, this sight is now commonplace in the Antarctic summer. Raising awareness of the continent is a good thing, but tourists can bring many dangers with them. If we are not careful, human presence in the area can damage the delicate ecosystem and destroy the natural environment.

Antarctica is less accessible than the Arctic and is still largely undamaged by humans. However, a hole in the **ozone layer** has been found above Antarctica. This was caused by gases that were used in refrigerators in the past, and indicates that human actions are having an effect on Antarctica, and the planet as a whole.

Due to both natural and human causes, the temperature of the Earth is rising—this is called climate change. The increased temperature is causing the polar ice to melt, which, in turn, contributes to sea levels rising. This will cause some coastal areas to become flooded, and people and animals to lose their homes.

Scientists have gained information about climate change from analysis of weather recordings, ice cores, and rocks and fossils. One way to combat climate change is to use renewable sources of energy, which will reduce the **emission** of **greenhouse gases**.

Reducing how much energy humans use is something that we can all help with. Just making a few small changes at home will contribute to keeping the global temperature down. For example, walking or cycling rather than using the car, and trying to use less electricity will make a huge improvement to our planet.

The research that scientists conduct in Antarctica is very important because it benefits the species that live there and also helps the rest of the world. By monitoring the ice and wildlife levels, scientists are able to predict how certain elements are going to affect the Earth in the future.

Scientists have also found that fish stocks in the Southern Ocean were being threatened by illegal and unregulated fishing. Some fishing companies trawled the waters and took more than their fair share of fish, trapping and killing many other creatures in the process. Scientists and **conservationists** have worked hard to stop this kind of fishing. Without their help, in the future there may no longer be a regular supply of fish in the Southern Ocean. The Southern Ocean is now strictly regulated by the Antarctic Treaty, and many people keep a close eye on the area, ensuring that its resources are not exploited.

The governments of many countries, such as Australia, Japan, Norway, South Africa, and the US, have taken on the task of preserving and protecting Antarctica. Thanks to their help, Antarctica is now a "nature preserve," meaning that it is protected and is a place devoted to peace and scientific research.

These governments brought the Antarctic Treaty into place to ensure that the environment was protected and that research had priority over all else. The treaty was signed in December 1959 after it was agreed upon by the 12 countries that were then active on the continent.

The objectives of the treaty are to keep the area free of military activity, nuclear testing, and radioactive waste, and ensure that it is used for peaceful purposes only. It encourages scientists from all countries to work together and use the area to conduct important research, and decrees that Antarctica cannot be owned by any one country.

There are now 50 countries that have signed the treaty and many of them will meet once a year to negotiate agreements and find new ways to keep Antarctica and its residents safe from harm.

Gazing at the pristine beauty of Antarctica, with its icebergs of cobalt blue and snow of pure white, is an experience that should be available to humans for generations to come. This paradise of piercing cold may hold the key to many questions about Earth's future, but it needs our help to endure and survive in close to pristine condition.

Far from civilization the fight for survival is tough, but there is hope on the ice-hardened horizon. With increasing numbers of people all around the world becoming aware of the changes happening at the poles, measures are being taken to protect it. Many people at home are making small changes to their lifestyles every day. The effects of these small gestures, from more and more people across the world can, over time, help reduce the impact of climate change in polar regions.

Understanding climate change and the many other threats that humans have put upon the planet is still a long way away, but

perseverance is key. Every generation needs new scientists and explorers to keep up the hard work that many pioneering individuals have started. New discoveries are made every single day and every footprint in the snow could be the start of something great.

How can you help to save Antarctica and its animals?

POLES APART:
FINDING THE SOUTH POLE

South Magnetic Pole: This is what the south needle on your compass points to. Think of the Earth as a giant magnet. The ends of this magnet with the strongest forces are the poles, which pull on the compass's needle. What makes the Earth magnetic is its fluid core. Because the fluid is constantly moving, the magnetic poles don't stay in the same place.

Geographic South Pole: This is at the southernmost point of the Earth. Imagine if there were a long stick stuck all the way through the planet at its axis—the point from which the Earth spins. This stick would therefore poke out at the Earth's Geographic North and South Poles.

Ceremonial South Pole: Located a short distance from the Geographic South Pole, the Ceremonial Pole is where explorers can get their pictures taken at the end of their journey. It is marked by a red-and-white-striped pole and is surrounded by flags of the Antarctic Treaty signatory countries.

The Antarctic Treaty is an agreement between 50 countries, which decided that Antarctica should be a protected area where scientific research has priority.

Pole locations

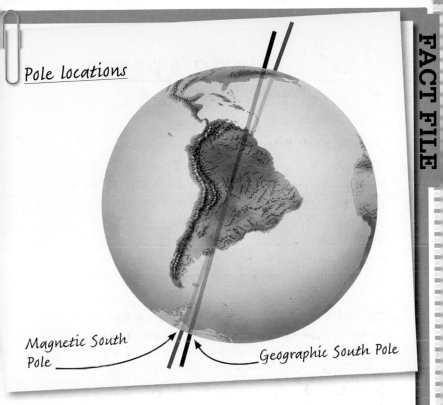

Magnetic South Pole

Geographic South Pole

Shifting ice

The marker for the Geographic Pole is situated on a moving sheet of ice that is more than 2 miles (3.2 km) thick. This sheet drifts about 30 ft (10 m) per year. This means that new markers need to be placed on the correct site once every year. Below are examples of a few of the markers at the Poles.

Geographic, 2011

Geographic, 2012

Ceremonial

NAVIGATION GAME

Navigating around Antarctica is not always an easy task in the snow. This means that being able to use a compass is essential for finding your way around. Use a compass and follow the directions below to take a tour of Antarctica. With some practice you will no longer be a navigating novice—you will learn how to be captain of the compass!

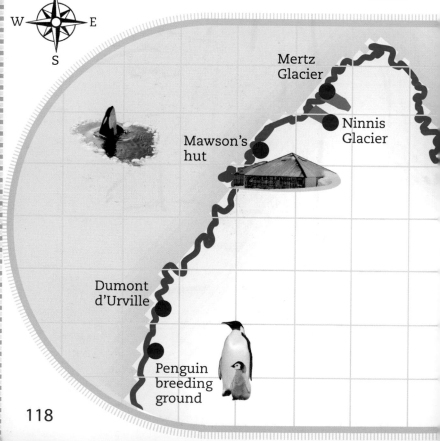

Mertz Glacier

Ninnis Glacier

Mawson's hut

Dumont d'Urville

Penguin breeding ground

← DIRECTIONS →

Start at McMurdo and look for the red dots.

1. Time for work! Travel south __ square(s) and east __ square(s) to reach the ice-core-drilling station.
2. Work's finished, and it's penguin breeding time! Travel __ square(s) south and __ square(s) west to see the penguin chicks.
3. One last stop before heading home—go __square(s) east and __square(s) north to visit Mawson's Hut.
4. Phew! What a long trip! Can you figure out how to get back to McMurdo?

Tip: Avoid the icy water!

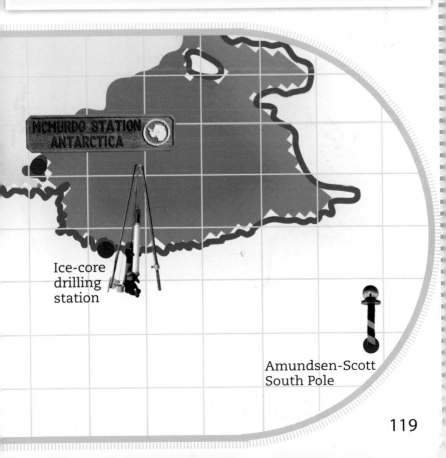

Ice-core drilling station

Amundsen-Scott South Pole

MAKE YOUR OWN COMPASS

If you'd like to try to find your way using a compass, you can make one of your own with a few simple materials.

WHAT YOU WILL NEED:

- large sewing needle
- magnet
- knife
- cork
- permanent-ink marker
- bowl

⚠️ WARNING!
Knives are sharp, so get an adult to help you.

1 With the hole, or eye, of the needle pointing downward, rub the magnet along the needle.

2 Using a knife, carefully slice a piece of cork.

3 Push the point of the magnetized needle through the sliced cork. Be careful!

4 Draw an arrow on the cork toward the point of the needle. This is your north point. Draw dots around the cork to show east, south, and west.

5 Half-fill a bowl with water and place it on a flat surface. Float the cork on the water. When the water has settled, the point of the needle will swing around to point north.

FACT:

A magnet will always point north and south, which is why if you were standing between the Geographic South Pole and the South Magnetic Pole, your compass would point in the wrong direction.

ANTARCTIC QUIZ

See if you can remember the answers to these questions about what you have read.

1. What does a paleontologist do?

2. When is the summer in Antarctica?

3. Why are dogs not allowed in Antarctica?

4. Where in the world do polar bears live?

5. How does ice form?

6. What is the name of Antarctica's most active volcano?

7. What is a crevasse?

8. What is the name for the condition a person has when they are cold, shivering, and struggling to breathe?

9. What is the name of the man from Douglas Mawson's expedition team who fell into the crevasse and died?

10. Who won the race to the pole in 1911?

11. What is the name of the food, made from ground meat and melted fat, that Antarctic explorers used to eat?

12. Which species of penguin grows the largest?

13. How can scientists find information about climate change?

14. What is a "nature preserve?"

15. How many countries have now signed the Antarctic Treaty?

Answers on page 125.

GLOSSARY

Acclimatize
Get used to a particular climate.

Adapt
Change something to better suit a certain condition or situation.

Biodegradable
When something can be slowly broken down into very small parts by natural processes.

Climate
Weather conditions in a certain area.

Conservationists
People who work to protect animals, plants, and the natural environment.

Continent
The main, large areas of land on the planet.

Deployed
To be sent out for a particular purpose.

Ecosystem
Community of plants and animals that interact and rely upon each other.

Emission
Sending something (such as a gas) out.

Extinction
When something, such as a plant or animal species, has died out completely.

Fatality
Disaster or accident that leads to a death.

Greenhouse Gases
Gases in the atmosphere that absorb heat, preventing it from escaping out into space. This causes the atmosphere to warm up.

Navigate
Find the way to get somewhere.

Ozone Layer
Layer of gas in the atmosphere that absorbs harmful ultraviolet radiation from the Sun.

Perseverance
Continuing to do something even though it is difficult.

Precipitation
Water that falls from the sky, e.g., rain, snow, sleet, or hail.

Rigorous
Strict or demanding.

Treacherous
Dangerous or difficult.

Answers to the Antarctic Quiz:
1. Studies fossils; 2. December to February; 3. People thought they were spreading diseases to the seals; 4. The Arctic; 5. By snow falling and getting squashed down; 6. Mount Erebus; 7. Crack in an ice sheet or glacier; 8. Hypothermia; 9. Belgrave Ninnis; 10. Roald Amundsen; 11. Pemmican; 12. Emperor Penguin; 13. From analysis of weather recordings, ice cores, and rocks and fossils; 14. A protected area; 15. 50.

INDEX

About the Author

Katy Lennon was born and raised in the UK where she spent a lot of her childhood reading as many books as she could get her hands on. She moved to the seaside town of Brighton to complete her degree and now enjoys being an editor at DK, helping to create books for young, inquiring minds. She lives in East London with three housemates and two cats and spends her spare time knitting, watching movies, reading, and listening to records on her dad's old record player.

About the Consultants

Dr. Linda Gambrell, Distinguished Professor of Education at Clemson University, has served as President of the National Reading Conference, the College Reading Association, and the International Reading Association. She is also reading consultant for the DK Readers.

Jamie Oliver is Publications & Education Manager at the British Antarctic Survey, the UK's national science operator in Antarctica. Jamie has managed award-winning educational resources about Antarctica and has spent time at Rothera Research Station in the Antarctic Peninsula. Jamie is also a Fellow of the Royal Geographical Society.

Have you read these other great books from DK?

Discover the fascinating world of creepy-crawlies in the Amazon.

Relive the drama of famous shipwrecks and survivors' stories.

Encounter the rare animals in the mountain forests of Cambodia.

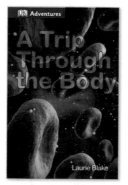

Be a rock detective! Look up close at rocks, minerals, and sparkling gems.

Explore the amazing systems at work inside the human body.

Step back nearly 20,000 years to the days of early cave dwellers.